This Ramadan Journal
Belongs To...
AF348873

Welcome to Your Ramadan Journal!

Hello! How fantastic that you will be joining us on this extraordinary journey through Ramadan! This journal is your magic book that will help you discover, learn, and celebrate this special month.

Ramadan is a time filled with amazing moments, where we learn about patience, sharing, and being better people. In this journal, you will find space to write down your thoughts and plans for each day of Ramadan. You will be able to record your experiences from this beautiful Holiday.

You can use this journal to write down everything that is important to you and that you want to remember about this unique time.

Prepare for an adventure full of joy, reflection, and fun. Are you ready to start your journey through Ramadan? Open this journal and begin creating your own, unique story!

It's me

My name is
I am...... years old
I live in.....
My signature

RAMADAN DAY 1

Check the box if you did it today.

Today I Prayed...

FAJR	DHUHR	ASR	MAGHRIB	ISHA
☐	☐	☐	☐	☐

Dhikr I Prayed Today...

HOW MANY ?

- ☐ **Subhanallah**
- ☐ **Alhamdulillah**
- ☐ **Allahu Akbar**
- ☐ **Lailahaillallah**
- ☐ **Durood**

I Woke Up for Suhoor

☐

I kept My Fast

☐

I Gave Charity

☐

I Prayed Quran

☐

Today I ...

- ☐ I performed a Dua for someone
- ☐ I thanked Allah
- ☐ Asked for forgiveness
- ☐ Performed a Sunnah
- ☐ Helped Someone in Need

RAMADAN REFLECTION DAY 1

Good Deeds I Did Today...

- [ ] _______________
- [ ] _______________
- [ ] _______________
- [ ] _______________
- [ ] _______________
- [ ] _______________

I Asked Allah For...

- [ ] _______________
- [ ] _______________
- [ ] _______________
- [ ] _______________
- [ ] _______________
- [ ] _______________

I Thanked Allah For...

- [ ] _______________
- [ ] _______________
- [ ] _______________
- [ ] _______________
- [ ] _______________
- [ ] _______________

I Need To Do More ...

- [ ] _______________
- [ ] _______________
- [ ] _______________
- [ ] _______________
- [ ] _______________
- [ ] _______________

RAMADAN DAY 2

Check the box if you did it today.

Today I Prayed...

FAJR	DHUHR	ASR	MAGHRIB	ISHA
☐	☐	☐	☐	☐

Dhikr I Prayed Today...

HOW MANY ?

☐ Subhanallah

☐ Alhamdulillah

☐ Allahu Akbar

☐ Lailahaillallah

☐ Durood

I Woke Up for Suhoor

☐

I kept My Fast

☐

I Gave Charity

☐

I Prayed Quran

☐

Today I ...

☐ I performed a Dua for someone

☐ I thanked Allah

☐ Asked for forgiveness

☐ Performed a Sunnah

☐ Helped Someone in Need

RAMADAN REFLECTION DAY 2

Good Deeds I Did Today...

- [ ] ______________________
- [ ] ______________________
- [ ] ______________________
- [ ] ______________________
- [ ] ______________________
- [ ] ______________________

I Asked Allah For...

- [ ] ______________________
- [ ] ______________________
- [ ] ______________________
- [ ] ______________________
- [ ] ______________________
- [ ] ______________________

I Thanked Allah For...

- [ ] ______________________
- [ ] ______________________
- [ ] ______________________
- [ ] ______________________
- [ ] ______________________
- [ ] ______________________

I Need To Do More ...

- [ ] ______________________
- [ ] ______________________
- [ ] ______________________
- [ ] ______________________
- [ ] ______________________
- [ ] ______________________

RAMADAN DAY 3

Check the box if you did it today.

Today I Prayed...

FAJR   DHUHR   ASR   MAGHRIB   ISHA

Dhikr I Prayed Today...

HOW MANY?

- Subhanallah
- Alhamdulillah
- Allahu Akbar
- Lailahaillallah
- Durood

I Woke Up for Suhoor

I kept My Fast

I Gave Charity

I Prayed Quran

Today I ...

- I performed a Dua for someo[ne]
- I thanked Allah
- Asked for forgiveness
- Performed a Sunnah
- Helped Someone in Need

RAMADAN REFLECTION DAY 3

Good Deeds I Did Today...

- [ ] ___________
- [ ] ___________
- [ ] ___________
- [ ] ___________
- [ ] ___________
- [ ] ___________

I Asked Allah For...

- [ ] ___________
- [ ] ___________
- [ ] ___________
- [ ] ___________
- [ ] ___________
- [ ] ___________

I Thanked Allah For...

- [ ] ___________
- [ ] ___________
- [ ] ___________
- [ ] ___________
- [ ] ___________
- [ ] ___________

I Need To Do More ...

- [ ] ___________
- [ ] ___________
- [ ] ___________
- [ ] ___________
- [ ] ___________
- [ ] ___________

RAMADAN DAY 4

Check the box if you did it today.

Today I Prayed...

FAJR ☐ DHUHR ☐ ASR ☐ MAGHRIB ☐ ISHA ☐

Dhikr I Prayed Today...

HOW MANY ?

☐ Subhanallah

☐ Alhamdulillah

☐ Allahu Akbar

☐ Lailahaillallah

☐ Durood

I Woke Up for Suhoor

☐

I kept My Fast

☐

I Gave Charity

☐

I Prayed Quran

☐

Today I ...

☐ I performed a Dua for someone

☐ I thanked Allah

☐ Asked for forgiveness

☐ Performed a Sunnah

☐ Helped Someone in Need

RAMADAN REFLECTION DAY 4

Good Deeds I Did Today...

- [ ] ___________
- [ ] ___________
- [ ] ___________
- [ ] ___________
- [ ] ___________
- [ ] ___________

I Asked Allah For...

- [ ] ___________
- [ ] ___________
- [ ] ___________
- [ ] ___________
- [ ] ___________
- [ ] ___________

I Thanked Allah For...

- [ ] ___________
- [ ] ___________
- [ ] ___________
- [ ] ___________
- [ ] ___________

I Need To Do More ...

- [ ] ___________
- [ ] ___________
- [ ] ___________
- [ ] ___________
- [ ] ___________

RAMADAN DAY 5

Check the box if you did it today.

Today I Prayed...

FAJR ☐ DHUHR ☐ ASR ☐ MAGHRIB ☐ ISHA ☐

Dhikr I Prayed Today...

HOW MANY ?

- ☐ Subhanallah
- ☐ Alhamdulillah
- ☐ Allahu Akbar
- ☐ Lailahaillallah
- ☐ Durood

I Woke Up for Suhoor

☐

I kept My Fast

☐

I Gave Charity

☐

I Prayed Quran

☐

Today I ...

- ☐ I performed a Dua for someon
- ☐ I thanked Allah
- ☐ Asked for forgiveness
- ☐ Performed a Sunnah
- ☐ Helped Someone in Need

RAMADAN REFLECTION DAY 5

Good Deeds I Did Today...

- [ ]
- [ ]
- [ ]
- [ ]
- [ ]
- [ ]

I Asked Allah For...

- [ ]
- [ ]
- [ ]
- [ ]
- [ ]
- [ ]

I Thanked Allah For...

- [ ]
- [ ]
- [ ]
- [ ]
- [ ]
- [ ]

I Need To Do More ...

- [ ]
- [ ]
- [ ]
- [ ]
- [ ]
- [ ]

RAMADAN DAY 6

Check the box if you did it today.

Today I Prayed...

FAJR ☐ DHUHR ☐ ASR ☐ MAGHRIB ☐ ISHA ☐

Dhikr I Prayed Today...

HOW MANY ?

☐ Subhanallah
☐ Alhamdulillah
☐ Allahu Akbar
☐ Lailahaillallah
☐ Durood

I Woke Up for Suhoor

☐

I Kept My Fast

☐

I Gave Charity

☐

I Prayed Quran

☐

Today I ...

☐ I performed a Dua for someone
☐ I thanked Allah
☐ Asked for forgiveness
☐ Performed a Sunnah
☐ Helped Someone in Need

RAMADAN REFLECTION DAY 6

Good Deeds I Did Today...

I Asked Allah For...

I Thanked Allah For...

I Need To Do More ...

RAMADAN DAY 7

Check the box if you did it today.

Today I Prayed...

FAJR	DHUHR	ASR	MAGHRIB	ISHA
☐	☐	☐	☐	☐

Dhikr I Prayed Today...

HOW MANY ?

☐ Subhanallah

☐ Alhamdulillah

☐ Allahu Akbar

☐ Lailahaillallah

☐ Durood

I Woke Up for Suhoor

☐

I Kept My Fast

☐

I Gave Charity

☐

I Prayed Quran

☐

Today I ...

☐ I performed a Dua for someon

☐ I thanked Allah

☐ Asked for forgiveness

☐ Performed a Sunnah

☐ Helped Someone in Need

RAMADAN REFLECTION DAY 7

Good Deeds I Did Today...

I Asked Allah For...

I Thanked Allah For...

I Need To Do More ...

RAMADAN DAY 8

Check the box if you did it today.

Today I Prayed...

FAJR ☐ DHUHR ☐ ASR ☐ MAGHRIB ☐ ISHA ☐

Dhikr I Prayed Today...

HOW MANY ?

☐ **Subhanallah**

☐ **Alhamdulillah**

☐ **Allahu Akbar**

☐ **Lailahaillallah**

☐ **Durood**

I Woke Up for Suhoor

☐

I Kept My Fast

☐

I Gave Charity

☐

I Prayed Quran

☐

Today I ...

☐ I performed a Dua for someone

☐ I thanked Allah

☐ Asked for forgiveness

☐ Performed a Sunnah

☐ Helped Someone in Need

RAMADAN REFLECTION DAY 8

Good Deeds I Did Today...

- ☐ _______________
- ☐ _______________
- ☐ _______________
- ☐ _______________
- ☐ _______________
- ☐ _______________

I Asked Allah For...

- ☐ _______________
- ☐ _______________
- ☐ _______________
- ☐ _______________
- ☐ _______________

I Thanked Allah For...

- ☐ _______________
- ☐ _______________
- ☐ _______________
- ☐ _______________
- ☐ _______________
- ☐ _______________

I Need To Do More ...

- ☐ _______________
- ☐ _______________
- ☐ _______________
- ☐ _______________
- ☐ _______________
- ☐ _______________

RAMADAN DAY 9

Check the box if you did it today.

Today I Prayed...

FAJR ☐ DHUHR ☐ ASR ☐ MAGHRIB ☐ ISHA ☐

Dhikr I Prayed Today...

HOW MANY ?

☐ Subhanallah

☐ Alhamdulillah

☐ Allahu Akbar

☐ Lailahaillallah

☐ Durood

I Woke Up for Suhoor

☐

I Kept My Fast

☐

I Gave Charity

☐

I Prayed Quran

☐

Today I ...

☐ I performed a Dua for someone

☐ I thanked Allah

☐ Asked for forgiveness

☐ Performed a Sunnah

☐ Helped Someone in Need

RAMADAN REFLECTION DAY 9

Good Deeds I Did Today...

- [ ] _______________
- [ ] _______________
- [ ] _______________
- [ ] _______________
- [ ] _______________
- [ ] _______________

I Asked Allah For...

- [ ] _______________
- [ ] _______________
- [ ] _______________
- [ ] _______________
- [ ] _______________
- [ ] _______________

I Thanked Allah For...

- [ ] _______________
- [ ] _______________
- [ ] _______________
- [ ] _______________
- [ ] _______________
- [ ] _______________

I Need To Do More ...

- [ ] _______________
- [ ] _______________
- [ ] _______________
- [ ] _______________
- [ ] _______________
- [ ] _______________

RAMADAN DAY 10

Check the box if you did it today.

Today I Prayed...

FAJR ☐ DHUHR ☐ ASR ☐ MAGHRIB ☐ ISHA ☐

Dhikr I Prayed Today...

HOW MANY ?

☐ Subhanallah

☐ Alhamdulillah

☐ Allahu Akbar

☐ Lailahaillallah

☐ Durood

I Woke Up for Suhoor

☐

I kept My Fast

☐

I Gave Charity

☐

I Prayed Quran

☐

Today I ...

☐ I performed a Dua for someone

☐ I thanked Allah

☐ Asked for forgiveness

☐ Performed a Sunnah

☐ Helped Someone in Need

RAMADAN REFLECTION DAY 10

Good Deeds I Did Today...

I Asked Allah For...

I Thanked Allah For...

I Need To Do More ...

RAMADAN DAY 11

Check the box if you did it today.

Today I Prayed...

FAJR DHUHR ASR MAGHRIB ISHA

Dhikr I Prayed Today...

HOW MANY ?

- Subhanallah
- Alhamdulillah
- Allahu Akbar
- Lailahaillallah
- Durood

I Woke Up for Suhoor

I Kept My Fast

I Gave Charity

I Prayed Quran

Today I ...

- I performed a Dua for someon
- I thanked Allah
- Asked for forgiveness
- Performed a Sunnah
- Helped Someone in Need

RAMADAN REFLECTION DAY 11

Good Deeds I Did Today...

I Asked Allah For...

I Thanked Allah For...

I Need To Do More ...

RAMADAN DAY 12

Check the box if you did it today.

Today I Prayed...

FAJR	DHUHR	ASR	MAGHRIB	ISHA
☐	☐	☐	☐	☐

Dhikr I Prayed Today...

HOW MANY?

- ☐ Subhanallah
- ☐ Alhamdulillah
- ☐ Allahu Akbar
- ☐ Lailahaillallah
- ☐ Durood

I Woke Up for Suhoor

☐

I Kept My Fast

☐

I Gave Charity

☐

I Prayed Quran

☐

Today I ...

- ☐ I performed a Dua for someone
- ☐ I thanked Allah
- ☐ Asked for forgiveness
- ☐ Performed a Sunnah
- ☐ Helped Someone in Need

RAMADAN REFLECTION DAY 12

Good Deeds I Did Today...

I Asked Allah For...

I Thanked Allah For...

I Need To Do More ...

RAMADAN DAY 13

Check the box if you did it today.

Today I Prayed...

FAJR	DHUHR	ASR	MAGHRIB	ISHA
☐	☐	☐	☐	☐

Dhikr I Prayed Today...

HOW MANY ?

- ☐ Subhanallah
- ☐ Alhamdulillah
- ☐ Allahu Akbar
- ☐ Lailahaillallah
- ☐ Durood

I Woke Up for Suhoor

☐

I kept My Fast

☐

I Gave Charity

☐

I Prayed Quran

☐

Today I ...

- ☐ I performed a Dua for someone
- ☐ I thanked Allah
- ☐ Asked for forgiveness
- ☐ Performed a Sunnah
- ☐ Helped Someone in Need

RAMADAN REFLECTION DAY 13

Good Deeds I Did Today...

- [ ] _______________
- [ ] _______________
- [ ] _______________
- [ ] _______________
- [ ] _______________
- [ ] _______________

I Asked Allah For...

- [ ] _______________
- [ ] _______________
- [ ] _______________
- [ ] _______________
- [ ] _______________
- [ ] _______________

I Thanked Allah For...

- [ ] _______________
- [ ] _______________
- [ ] _______________
- [ ] _______________
- [ ] _______________
- [ ] _______________

I Need To Do More ...

- [ ] _______________
- [ ] _______________
- [ ] _______________
- [ ] _______________
- [ ] _______________

RAMADAN DAY 14

Check the box if you did it today.

Today I Prayed...

FAJR	DHUHR	ASR	MAGHRIB	ISHA
☐	☐	☐	☐	☐

Dhikr I Prayed Today...

HOW MANY ?

☐ Subhanallah

☐ Alhamdulillah

☐ Allahu Akbar

☐ Lailahaillallah

☐ Durood

I Woke Up for Suhoor

☐

I Kept My Fast

☐

I Gave Charity

☐

I Prayed Quran

☐

Today I ...

☐ I performed a Dua for someone

☐ I thanked Allah

☐ Asked for forgiveness

☐ Performed a Sunnah

☐ Helped Someone in Need

RAMADAN REFLECTION DAY 14

Good Deeds I Did Today...

I Asked Allah For...

I Thanked Allah For...

I Need To Do More ...

RAMADAN DAY 15

Check the box if you did it today.

Today I Prayed...

FAJR	DHUHR	ASR	MAGHRIB	ISHA
☐	☐	☐	☐	☐

Dhikr I Prayed Today...

HOW MANY ?

- ☐ Subhanallah
- ☐ Alhamdulillah
- ☐ Allahu Akbar
- ☐ Lailahaillallah
- ☐ Durood

I Woke Up for Suhoor

☐

I kept My Fast

☐

I Gave Charity

☐

I Prayed Quran

☐

Today I ...

- ☐ I performed a Dua for someone
- ☐ I thanked Allah
- ☐ Asked for forgiveness
- ☐ Performed a Sunnah
- ☐ Helped Someone in Need

RAMADAN REFLECTION DAY 15

Good Deeds I Did Today...

I Asked Allah For...

I Thanked Allah For...

I Need To Do More ...

RAMADAN DAY 16

Check the box if you did it today.

Today I Prayed...

FAJR DHUHR ASR MAGHRIB ISHA

Dhikr I Prayed Today...

HOW MANY ?

- Subhanallah
- Alhamdulillah
- Allahu Akbar
- Lailahaillallah
- Durood

I Woke Up for Suhoor

I kept My Fast

I Gave Charity

I Prayed Quran

Today I ...

- I performed a Dua for someone
- I thanked Allah
- Asked for forgiveness
- Performed a Sunnah
- Helped Someone in Need

RAMADAN REFLECTION DAY 16

Good Deeds I Did Today...

I Asked Allah For...

I Thanked Allah For...

I Need To Do More ...

RAMADAN DAY 17

Check the box if you did it today.

Today I Prayed...

FAJR	DHUHR	ASR	MAGHRIB	ISHA
☐	☐	☐	☐	☐

Dhikr I Prayed Today...

HOW MANY ?

- ☐ Subhanallah
- ☐ Alhamdulillah
- ☐ Allahu Akbar
- ☐ Lailahaillallah
- ☐ Durood

I Woke Up for Suhoor

☐

I kept My Fast

☐

I Gave Charity

☐

I Prayed Quran

☐

Today I ...

- ☐ I performed a Dua for someone
- ☐ I thanked Allah
- ☐ Asked for forgiveness
- ☐ Performed a Sunnah
- ☐ Helped Someone in Need

RAMADAN REFLECTION DAY 17

Good Deeds I Did Today...

- [ ] _______________
- [ ] _______________
- [ ] _______________
- [ ] _______________
- [ ] _______________
- [ ] _______________

I Asked Allah For...

- [ ] _______________
- [ ] _______________
- [ ] _______________
- [ ] _______________
- [ ] _______________
- [ ] _______________

I Thanked Allah For...

- [ ] _______________
- [ ] _______________
- [ ] _______________
- [ ] _______________
- [ ] _______________

I Need To Do More ...

- [ ] _______________
- [ ] _______________
- [ ] _______________
- [ ] _______________
- [ ] _______________

RAMADAN DAY 18

Check the box if you did it today.

Today I Prayed...

FAJR ☐ DHUHR ☐ ASR ☐ MAGHRIB ☐ ISHA ☐

Dhikr I Prayed Today...

HOW MANY ?

☐ Subhanallah
☐ Alhamdulillah
☐ Allahu Akbar
☐ Lailahaillallah
☐ Durood

I Woke Up for Suhoor

☐

I kept My Fast

☐

I Gave Charity

☐

I Prayed Quran

☐

Today I ...

☐ I performed a Dua for someone
☐ I thanked Allah
☐ Asked for forgiveness
☐ Performed a Sunnah
☐ Helped Someone in Need

RAMADAN REFLECTION DAY 18

Good Deeds I Did Today...

I Asked Allah For...

I Thanked Allah For...

I Need To Do More ...

RAMADAN DAY 19

Check the box if you did it today.

Today I Prayed...

FAJR	DHUHR	ASR	MAGHRIB	ISHA
☐	☐	☐	☐	☐

Dhikr I Prayed Today...

HOW MANY ?

- ☐ Subhanallah
- ☐ Alhamdulillah
- ☐ Allahu Akbar
- ☐ Lailahaillallah
- ☐ Durood

I Woke Up for Suhoor
☐

I kept My Fast
☐

I Gave Charity
☐

I Prayed Quran
☐

Today I ...

- ☐ I performed a Dua for someone
- ☐ I thanked Allah
- ☐ Asked for forgiveness
- ☐ Performed a Sunnah
- ☐ Helped Someone in Need

RAMADAN REFLECTION DAY 19

Good Deeds I Did Today...

- [ ] __________________
- [ ] __________________
- [ ] __________________
- [ ] __________________
- [ ] __________________
- [ ] __________________

I Asked Allah For...

- [ ] __________________
- [ ] __________________
- [ ] __________________
- [ ] __________________
- [ ] __________________
- [ ] __________________

I Thanked Allah For...

- [ ] __________________
- [ ] __________________
- [ ] __________________
- [ ] __________________
- [ ] __________________
- [ ] __________________

I Need To Do More ...

- [ ] __________________
- [ ] __________________
- [ ] __________________
- [ ] __________________
- [ ] __________________
- [ ] __________________

RAMADAN DAY 20

Check the box if you did it today.

Today I Prayed...

FAJR   DHUHR   ASR   MAGHRIB   ISHA

Dhikr I Prayed Today...

HOW MANY ?

- Subhanallah
- Alhamdulillah
- Allahu Akbar
- Lailahaillallah
- Durood

I Woke Up for Suhoor

I kept My Fast

I Gave Charity

I Prayed Quran

Today I ...

- I performed a Dua for someone
- I thanked Allah
- Asked for forgiveness
- Performed a Sunnah
- Helped Someone in Need

RAMADAN REFLECTION DAY 20

Good Deeds I Did Today...

I Asked Allah For...

I Thanked Allah For...

I Need To Do More ...

RAMADAN DAY 21

Check the box if you did it today.

Today I Prayed...

FAJR ☐ DHUHR ☐ ASR ☐ MAGHRIB ☐ ISHA ☐

Dhikr I Prayed Today...

HOW MANY ?

☐ Subhanallah

☐ Alhamdulillah

☐ Allahu Akbar

☐ Lailahaillallah

☐ Durood

I Woke Up for Suhoor

☐

I kept My Fast

☐

I Gave Charity

☐

I Prayed Quran

☐

Today I ...

☐ I performed a Dua for someone

☐ I thanked Allah

☐ Asked for forgiveness

☐ Performed a Sunnah

☐ Helped Someone in Need

RAMADAN REFLECTION DAY 21

Good Deeds I Did Today...

- [ ] ___________
- [ ] ___________
- [ ] ___________
- [ ] ___________
- [ ] ___________
- [ ] ___________

I Asked Allah For...

- [ ] ___________
- [ ] ___________
- [ ] ___________
- [ ] ___________
- [ ] ___________
- [ ] ___________

I Thanked Allah For...

- [ ] ___________
- [ ] ___________
- [ ] ___________
- [ ] ___________
- [ ] ___________
- [ ] ___________

I Need To Do More ...

- [ ] ___________
- [ ] ___________
- [ ] ___________
- [ ] ___________
- [ ] ___________

RAMADAN DAY 22

Check the box if you did it today.

Today I Prayed...

FAJR ☐ DHUHR ☐ ASR ☐ MAGHRIB ☐ ISHA ☐

Dhikr I Prayed Today...

HOW MANY ?

☐ Subhanallah

☐ Alhamdulillah

☐ Allahu Akbar

☐ Lailahaillallah

☐ Durood

I Woke Up for Suhoor

☐

I Kept My Fast

☐

I Gave Charity

☐

I Prayed Quran

☐

Today I ...

☐ I performed a Dua for someone

☐ I thanked Allah

☐ Asked for forgiveness

☐ Performed a Sunnah

☐ Helped Someone in Need

RAMADAN REFLECTION DAY 22

Good Deeds I Did Today...

- [ ] _______________
- [ ] _______________
- [ ] _______________
- [ ] _______________
- [ ] _______________
- [ ] _______________

I Asked Allah For...

- [ ] _______________
- [ ] _______________
- [ ] _______________
- [ ] _______________
- [ ] _______________
- [ ] _______________

I Thanked Allah For...

- [ ] _______________
- [ ] _______________
- [ ] _______________
- [ ] _______________
- [ ] _______________

I Need To Do More ...

- [ ] _______________
- [ ] _______________
- [ ] _______________
- [ ] _______________
- [ ] _______________

RAMADAN DAY 23

Check the box if you did it today.

Today I Prayed...

FAJR ☐
DHUHR ☐
ASR ☐
MAGHRIB ☐
ISHA ☐

Dhikr I Prayed Today...

HOW MANY ?

☐ Subhanallah
☐ Alhamdulillah
☐ Allahu Akbar
☐ Lailahaillallah
☐ Durood

I Woke Up for Suhoor
☐

I kept My Fast
☐

I Gave Charity
☐

I Prayed Quran
☐

Today I ...
☐ I performed a Dua for someone
☐ I thanked Allah
☐ Asked for forgiveness
☐ Performed a Sunnah
☐ Helped Someone in Need

RAMADAN REFLECTION DAY 23

Good Deeds I Did Today...

- [ ] ______________________
- [ ] ______________________
- [ ] ______________________
- [ ] ______________________
- [ ] ______________________
- [ ] ______________________

I Asked Allah For...

- [ ] ______________________
- [ ] ______________________
- [ ] ______________________
- [ ] ______________________
- [ ] ______________________
- [ ] ______________________

I Thanked Allah For...

- [ ] ______________________
- [ ] ______________________
- [ ] ______________________
- [ ] ______________________
- [ ] ______________________

I Need To Do More ...

- [ ] ______________________
- [ ] ______________________
- [ ] ______________________
- [ ] ______________________
- [ ] ______________________

RAMADAN DAY 24

Check the box if you did it today.

Today I Prayed...

FAJR	DHUHR	ASR	MAGHRIB	ISHA
☐	☐	☐	☐	☐

Dhikr I Prayed Today...

HOW MANY ?

☐ Subhanallah

☐ Alhamdulillah

☐ Allahu Akbar

☐ Lailahaillallah

☐ Durood

I Woke Up for Suhoor

☐

I kept My Fast

☐

I Gave Charity

☐

I Prayed Quran

☐

Today I ...

☐ I performed a Dua for someone

☐ I thanked Allah

☐ Asked for forgiveness

☐ Performed a Sunnah

☐ Helped Someone in Need

RAMADAN REFLECTION DAY 24

Good Deeds I Did Today...

I Asked Allah For...

I Thanked Allah For...

I Need To Do More ...

RAMADAN DAY 25

Check the box if you did it today.

Today I Prayed...

FAJR	DHUHR	ASR	MAGHRIB	ISHA
☐	☐	☐	☐	☐

Dhikr I Prayed Today...

HOW MANY?

- ☐ Subhanallah
- ☐ Alhamdulillah
- ☐ Allahu Akbar
- ☐ Lailahaillallah
- ☐ Durood

I Woke Up for Suhoor

☐

I Kept My Fast

☐

I Gave Charity

☐

I Prayed Quran

☐

Today I ...

- ☐ I performed a Dua for someone
- ☐ I thanked Allah
- ☐ Asked for forgiveness
- ☐ Performed a Sunnah
- ☐ Helped Someone in Need

RAMADAN REFLECTION DAY 25

Good Deeds I Did Today...

I Asked Allah For...

I Thanked Allah For...

I Need To Do More ...

RAMADAN DAY 26

Check the box if you did it today.

Today I Prayed...

FAJR DHUHR ASR MAGHRIB ISHA

Dhikr I Prayed Today...

HOW MANY ?

- Subhanallah
- Alhamdulillah
- Allahu Akbar
- Lailahaillallah
- Durood

I Woke Up for Suhoor

I kept My Fast

I Gave Charity

I Prayed Quran

Today I ...

- I performed a Dua for someone
- I thanked Allah
- Asked for forgiveness
- Performed a Sunnah
- Helped Someone in Need

RAMADAN REFLECTION DAY 26

Good Deeds I Did Today...

I Asked Allah For...

I Thanked Allah For...

I Need To Do More ...

RAMADAN DAY 27

Check the box if you did it today.

Today I Prayed...

FAJR	DHUHR	ASR	MAGHRIB	ISHA
☐	☐	☐	☐	☐

Dhikr I Prayed Today...

HOW MANY?

- ☐ Subhanallah
- ☐ Alhamdulillah
- ☐ Allahu Akbar
- ☐ Lailahaillallah
- ☐ Durood

I Woke Up for Suhoor

☐

I kept My Fast

☐

I Gave Charity

☐

I Prayed Quran

☐

Today I ...

- ☐ I performed a Dua for someone
- ☐ I thanked Allah
- ☐ Asked for forgiveness
- ☐ Performed a Sunnah
- ☐ Helped Someone in Need

RAMADAN REFLECTION DAY 27

Good Deeds I Did Today...

- [ ] ________________
- [ ] ________________
- [ ] ________________
- [ ] ________________
- [ ] ________________
- [ ] ________________

I Asked Allah For...

- [ ] ________________
- [ ] ________________
- [ ] ________________
- [ ] ________________
- [ ] ________________
- [ ] ________________

I Thanked Allah For...

- [ ] ________________
- [ ] ________________
- [ ] ________________
- [ ] ________________
- [ ] ________________
- [ ] ________________

I Need To Do More ...

- [ ] ________________
- [ ] ________________
- [ ] ________________
- [ ] ________________
- [ ] ________________
- [ ] ________________

RAMADAN DAY 28

Check the box if you did it today.

Today I Prayed...

FAJR DHUHR ASR MAGHRIB ISHA

Dhikr I Prayed Today...

HOW MANY ?

- Subhanallah
- Alhamdulillah
- Allahu Akbar
- Lailahaillallah
- Durood

I Woke Up for Suhoor

I kept My Fast

I Gave Charity

I Prayed Quran

Today I ...

- I performed a Dua for someone
- I thanked Allah
- Asked for forgiveness
- Performed a Sunnah
- Helped Someone in Need

RAMADAN REFLECTION DAY 28

Good Deeds I Did Today...

I Asked Allah For...

I Thanked Allah For...

I Need To Do More ...

RAMADAN DAY 29

Check the box if you did it today.

Today I Prayed...

FAJR DHUHR ASR MAGHRIB ISHA

Dhikr I Prayed Today...

HOW MANY ?

- Subhanallah
- Alhamdulillah
- Allahu Akbar
- Lailahaillallah
- Durood

I Woke Up for Suhoor

I kept My Fast

I Gave Charity

I Prayed Quran

Today I ...

- I performed a Dua for someone
- I thanked Allah
- Asked for forgiveness
- Performed a Sunnah
- Helped Someone in Need

RAMADAN REFLECTION DAY 29

Good Deeds I Did Today...

I Asked Allah For...

I Thanked Allah For...

I Need To Do More ...

RAMADAN DAY 30

Check the box if you did it today.

Today I Prayed...

FAJR	DHUHR	ASR	MAGHRIB	ISHA
☐	☐	☐	☐	☐

Dhikr I Prayed Today...

HOW MANY ?

- ☐ Subhanallah
- ☐ Alhamdulillah
- ☐ Allahu Akbar
- ☐ Lailahaillallah
- ☐ Durood

I Woke Up for Suhoor

☐

I kept My Fast

☐

I Gave Charity

☐

I Prayed Quran

☐

Today I ...

- ☐ I performed a Dua for someone
- ☐ I thanked Allah
- ☐ Asked for forgiveness
- ☐ Performed a Sunnah
- ☐ Helped Someone in Need

RAMADAN REFLECTION DAY 30

Good Deeds I Did Today...

- [ ] _______________
- [ ] _______________
- [ ] _______________
- [ ] _______________
- [ ] _______________
- [ ] _______________

I Asked Allah For...

- [ ] _______________
- [ ] _______________
- [ ] _______________
- [ ] _______________
- [ ] _______________
- [ ] _______________

I Thanked Allah For...

- [ ] _______________
- [ ] _______________
- [ ] _______________
- [ ] _______________
- [ ] _______________
- [ ] _______________

I Need To Do More ...

- [ ] _______________
- [ ] _______________
- [ ] _______________
- [ ] _______________
- [ ] _______________
- [ ] _______________

Weekly Plan

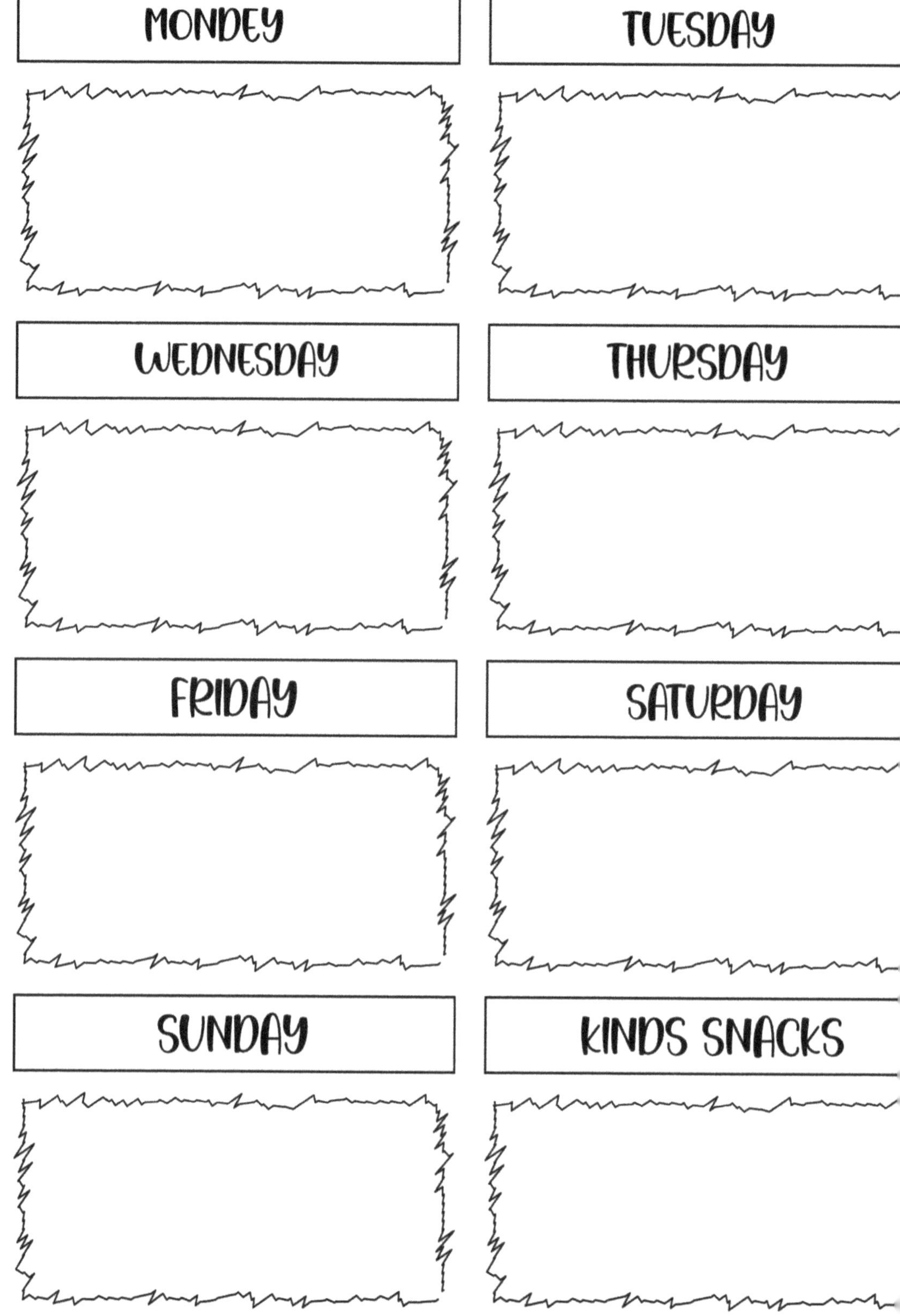

RAMADAN WEEK 1

DAYS	SUHOOR	IFTAR
MONDEY		
TUESDAY		
WEDNESDAY		
THURSDAY		
FRIDAY		
SATURDAY		
SUNDAY		

NOTES

RAMADAN WEEK 2

DAYS	SUHOOR	IFTAR
MONDEY		
TUESDAY		
WEDNESDAY		
THURSDAY		
FRIDAY		
SATURDAY		
SUNDAY		

NOTES

RAMADAN WEEK 3

DAYS	SUHOOR	IFTAR
MONDEY		
TUESDAY		
WEDNESDAY		
THURSDAY		
FRIDAY		
SATURDAY		
SUNDAY		

NOTES

RAMADAN WEEK 4

DAYS	SUHOOR	IFTAR
MONDEY		
TUESDAY		
WEDNESDAY		
THURSDAY		
FRIDAY		
SATURDAY		
SUNDAY		

NOTES

Recipe for Fruity overnight oatmeal on Suhoor

Ingredients:

1 cup of rolled oats

1 cup of milk (plant-based milk can be used for a lactose-free option)

1 tablespoon of honey or maple syrup (optional)

Fresh fruits like banana, blueberries, strawberries (chopped)

A handful of nuts or almonds (optional)

1 cup of plain yogurt

Instructions:

In a small bowl, mix the rolled oats with milk. Leave in the refrigerator overnight so the oats soften and absorb the milk.

In the morning, add yogurt and honey/maple syrup to the oat mixture. Mix well.

Top with fresh fruits and sprinkle with nuts/almonds for extra texture and nutrition.

Serve immediately, providing a tasty and nutritious meal for suhoor.

This meal is great for kids as it's sweet yet healthy, and the addition of fruits and nuts provides vitamins, minerals, and healthy fats. Oats are high in fiber, which will help keep them full for a longer period.

Recipe for Chicken with Rice and Vegetable for Iftar

Ingredients:

2 chicken breasts, cut into cubes

1 cup of basmati rice

2 cups of chicken broth or water

1 carrot, diced

1 red bell pepper, diced

1 small onion, chopped

2 tablespoons of vegetable oil

1 teaspoon of turmeric

Salt and pepper to taste

Fresh herbs (e.g., parsley, cilantro) for garnish

Instructions:

Heat the oil in a pan and add the onion. Sauté until translucent.

Add the chicken and cook until fully done.

Add the carrot and bell pepper, and sauté for a few minutes.

Add the rice and turmeric, stirring everything together well.

Pour in the chicken broth or water, cover, and cook on low heat until the rice absorbs all the liquid and is soft.

Season with salt and pepper to taste.

Garnish with fresh herbs before serving.

This meal is great for kids as it's flavorful yet simple and mild. Chicken provides protein, rice supplies carbohydrates, and vegetables are a source of vitamins and minerals. It's a balanced and satisfying meal for iftar.

EID PREPARATION

GIFT TO BUY

CHOOSE NEW OUTFITS

DECORATE YOUR ROOM

PLAN YOUR FAVORITE MEAL

EID PREPARATION

BAKE COOKIES

WRITE EID CARDS

CREATE A GIFT LIST

LEARN EID SONGS

EID PREPARATION

MAKE DECORATIONS

CHOOSE GAMES TO PLAY

PLAN A MOVIE NIGHT

HELP WITH COOKING

EID PREPARATION

PLAN A FAMILY TRIP

PREPARE A PERFORMANCE

ORGANIZE A TOY SWAP

MAKE A THANKFULNESS LIST

EID PREPARATION

CHOOSE A CHARITY PROJECT

LEARN ABOUT EID TRADITIONS

PREPARE FOR AN EID PHOTO SCAVENGER HUNT

SET GOALS FOR AFTER EID

NOTES

NOTES

NOTES

NOTES

NOTES

NOTES

NOTES

NOTES

NOTES

NOTES

NOTES

Thank You for Completing Your Ramadan Journal

Dear Friend,

Wow, what an incredible journey we have had this Ramadan together! Now, as it comes to an end, we want to thank you for being part of this wonderful journey.

Thank you for every page you filled, every story you shared, and every smile you gave us. Your enthusiasm, creativity, and determination made this Ramadan truly special.

Remember, each day of Ramadan was another chance to learn something new and to be a better version of yourself. We are so proud of how beautifully you understood and lived this.

We hope this journal remains a keepsake full of precious memories and lessons you took from this amazing month. And remember, every new day is an opportunity to continue these beautiful traditions.

Thank you for being with us. See you next year for another incredible adventure!

www.ingramcontent.com/pod-product-compliance
Lightning Source LLC
LaVergne TN
LVHW070041070726
842759LV00036B/1111